WHERE IS GOD WHEN THINGS GO WRONG?

JOHN BLANCHARD

EP EVANGELICAL PRESS

EVANGELICAL PRESS
Faverdale North Industrial Estate, Darlington, DL3 0PH, England

Evangelical Press USA
P. O. Box 825, Webster, New York 14580, USA

e-mail: sales@evangelicalpress.org

web: http://www.evangelicalpress.org

First published 2005

British Library Cataloguing in Publication Data available

ISBN 0 85234 590 9

Printed in the United States of America.

**Life could hardly have been better for
the beautiful American teenager as she
prepared to dive into the sparkling waters
of Chesapeake Bay...**

Her father had come through the nation's Great Depression by skilfully building things 'from stuff others threw away', eventually becoming a successful businessman and on the United States wrestling team at the 1932 Olympic Games held in Los Angeles.

With her three sisters she had assimilated their father's secure core values, while delightful family holidays, sports (she was captain of the girls' lacrosse team at her school) and a place in the school's Honour Society were seamless parts of her serene teenage years. In her own words, 'As far back as I could remember, there had been nothing but happiness surrounding our lives and home.' To cap it all, God also seemed to be on board. Churchgoing was almost as natural to her as breathing and in her mid-teens she had professed herself a committed Christian.

She must have felt on top of the world. Now, as the sun was setting at the end of that hot July day, she anticipated the thrill of knifing through the cool, refreshing water. She flexed her suntanned arms and legs and dived in. Five seconds later her life had changed for ever…

As she turned back towards the surface, her head struck a rock, trapping her on the sandy floor of the bay. Sprawling out of control, she felt 'something like an electric shock, combined with a vibration — like a heavy metal spring being suddenly and sharply uncoiled'. She desperately tried to fight her way to the surface, but her arms and legs failed to respond to the frantic messages from her brain. When she could hardly hold her breath any longer, a tidal swell lifted her part of the way up. Her sister Kathy reached down to grasp her and with the help of others manoeuvred her onto dry land.

An ambulance rushed her to hospital and as the siren wailed she tried to fight her fear with long-remembered verses from the Bible: 'The Lord is my Shepherd, I shall not be in want. He makes me lie down in green pastures…' In the emergency room, confused, frightened and feeling queasy from the usual hospital smells, she again reached out to Scripture: 'Even though I walk through the valley of the shadow of death, I will fear no evil, for you are with me…'

After a series of tests and X-rays, doctors performed emergency surgery on her head. The next days were spent drifting in and out of consciousness while strapped into a Stryker Frame, a canvas 'sandwich' which allowed her to be turned over every two hours without individual parts of her body being moved. Her conscious hours were punctuated by fear and pain and her unconscious ones by terrifying dreams and drug-induced hallucinations.

A bone scan and a myelogram followed, then delicate surgery to offset the damage caused by a fracture-dislocation of the spine, but eventually the doctors faced her with the facts: she was a total quadriplegic. In layman's language, injury to her spinal cord meant that she would never again be able to use her arms, hands or legs.

She was utterly devastated. The weeks that followed included fleeting moments of hope as the doctors suggested various forms of treatment and therapy, but they were soon shut out by bitter resentment:

'Oh, God, how can you do this to me?'

'What have you done to me?'

'What's the use of believing when your prayers fall on deaf ears?'

'God doesn't care. He doesn't even care.'

Grief, remorse and depression swept over her 'like a thick, choking blanket … the mental and spiritual anguish was as unbearable as the physical torture… How I wished for strength and control enough in my fingers to do something, anything, to end my life!' Earlier years of spiritual security now seemed a mocking background to one inescapable question: 'Where is God when things go wrong?'

The question goes back thousands of years and the argument behind it can be summarized like this:

1. Evil and suffering exist in the world.
2. If God were all-powerful, he could prevent evil and suffering.
3. If he were all-loving, he would want to prevent these.
4. If there were an all-powerful, all-loving God, there would be no evil and suffering in the world.
5. God is therefore powerless, loveless or non-existent.

God in the dock

The logic seems pretty watertight and the case against God even stronger when we read what the Bible says about him. It claims not only that he is 'God of gods and Lord of lords … mighty and awesome' (Deuteronomy 10:17) and 'works out everything in conformity with the purpose of his will' (Ephesians 1:11), but that he is 'compassionate and gracious, slow to anger, abounding in love' (Psalm 103:8). At first glance it seems impossible to reconcile these statements with what is happening every day in the world around us and, as we know that catastrophes, accidents, disease, evil, pain, suffering and death are *facts* (someone has said, 'The history of the human race is nothing less

The history of the human race is nothing less than the history of suffering.

than the history of suffering'), many think it logical to conclude that God is non-existent. The contemporary apologist Ravi Zacharias says, 'I have never defended the existence of God at a university without being asked about this question of evil in the world.'

For some people, the question arises in a moment of terrible trauma. During the ruthless 'ethnic cleansing' of Kosovo in the late 1990s, one woman told the news media of soldiers separating ten women from their families and raping them by the roadside. As they did so, they sneered, 'We are not going to shoot you, but we want your families to see what we are doing.' Telling her story to reporters, she added, 'It was then that I came to know that God does not exist.' This was not a formal declaration of philosophical atheism, but a passionate cry from the heart, one that many others have shared in moments of searing pain. Hard-core atheists turn the question into a creed: 'There is no God; and evil and suffering prove it.'

In contemporary usage 'evil' is a broad term describing anything that is seen as bad or harmful. This covers two main categories: on

the one hand, naturally occurring events which cause harm and suffering, and on the other, morally reprehensible human behaviour. We could cite countless examples of both.

Natural disasters

Suffering which is attributable to natural causes is most easily thought of in terms of natural disasters, and a few outstanding examples speak for thousands of others.

- In 1319 the fallout from the Mount Etna volcano killed 15,000 in the town of Catania.
- In 1755 the terrifying Lisbon earthquake virtually wiped out the entire city. The effects were so widespread that the waters in Scotland's Loch Lomond rose and fell several feet every ten minutes for an hour and a half.
- In 1923 some 160,000 people perished in Japan when earthquakes struck Tokyo and Yokohama.

How do these events square with the Bible's claim that 'In [God's] hand are the depths of the earth, and the mountain peaks belong to him'? (Psalm 95:4).

- In 1953 a record spring tide wreaked havoc on both sides of the North Sea, killing nearly 2,000 people in Holland and over 300 in England.
- When Hurricane Mitch, dubbed 'the storm of the century', hit South America in 1998, 12,000 people were drowned or crushed to death and millions left homeless following torrential rain and winds of up to 150 miles per hour.
- In the last major natural disaster of the twentieth century some 30,000 people perished when freak rains hit Venezuela in December 1999.
- Just five years later, the whole world was shaken by an even greater catastrophe…

WHERE IS GOD WHEN THINGS GO WRONG?

Tsunami!

At 7.58 a.m. local time on 26 December 2004, tectonic plates several miles under the sea off the north-western tip of the Indonesian archipelago sprang apart with the force of more than 1,000 atomic bombs, triggering thirty-six earthquakes, displacing trillions of tons of water and realigning a 600-mile section of the Indian Ocean's seabed. The biggest earthquake registered 9.0 on the Richter scale and the massive upheaval of water generated a tsunami, a long, high sea wave that began to race across the ocean at over 500 miles per hour.

Twenty minutes later five colossal waves laid waste the market town of Banda Aceh in Sumatra. Thousands perished; less than 100 survived. Elsewhere in Indonesia, the busy town of Lhuknga was scoured off the face of the earth by a black wall of water twice as high as its palm trees. Only a few dozen of Lhuknga's 10,000 inhabitants escaped the deluge. The official Indonesian death toll eventually reached well over 220,000. As it roared across the Indian Ocean, the tsunami overwhelmed the Andaman and Nicobar islands, sweeping 7,000 people to death.

In eighty minutes it had reached the coast of Thailand, where luxury resorts like Phuket, Koh Lanta, Koh Phi Phi and Krabi lay directly in its path. The result was almost beyond description. Moments earlier holidaymakers had been strolling along the beaches while babies slept in their cots and patients in hospital beds. Businessmen, housewives and others were going about their day's work. Suddenly, with no more than a few moments' warning, a succession of stupendous waves changed their world for ever. One survivor said, 'It was as if someone had pulled out the plug to the earth.' Hotels, guest houses, homes and offices collapsed like packs of cards. Motor vehicles were tossed into nearby trees as if they were matchbox models. Over 5,000 people died.

In another twenty minutes the tsunami hit Sri Lanka, devastating the seaside town of Galle and the nearby coastline. Within minutes thousands of corpses littered the streets and beaches. Survivors clung desperately to trees and buildings while a raging torrent of water swept past them, carrying a ghastly cargo of debris and drowned animals, along with countless human bodies, some of

8

them gashed open or dismembered by the force of the water. The eight coaches of a crowded train were hurled from the tracks and flung into nearby trees like unwanted toys; there were 1,000 passengers; only a handful survived. Of well over 46,000 deaths in Sri Lanka, at least 15,000 were children.

Two hours after the initial earthquake, the wall of water had crossed the Bay of Bengal and ripped into the islands and towns of India's east coast, claiming over 10,000 lives, including an entire church congregation gathered for morning worship. Seven hours after the earthquake, gigantic waves swamped Male, the capital of the Maldives, most of whose 1,190 islands are only a few feet above sea level. Fourteen islands were flattened and nearly 100 people drowned. An hour later and the waves hit the east coast of Africa, killing over 200 people in Somalia, Kenya and Tanzania.

Four weeks on, the tsunami's official death toll was put at over 280,000, but the true figure may never be known. A United Nations spokesman said that, in terms of the area affected, this was the greatest natural catastrophe in the world's history. *The Independent* rightly called it 'the wave that shook the world' — some of Asia's islands shifted their positions by several metres, both laterally and vertically; in Great Britain, over 7,500 miles away from the epicentre, the earth moved to a measurable extent; and geologists right around the world registered vibrations.

It shook the world in other ways, too. A *Daily Telegraph* editorial admitted, 'Our brains are not designed to compute suffering on such a scale ... the swallowing up of whole communities is literally unimaginable.' United States President George W. Bush said that the event 'brought loss and grief to the world beyond our comprehension'.

But how can this appalling disaster, and the others mentioned earlier, be reconciled with the Bible's assurance that 'The LORD does whatever pleases him, in the heavens and on the earth, in the seas and all their depths', and its insistence that '... ocean depths ... do his bidding'? (Psalms 135:6; 148:7). A *Daily Telegraph* reader answered for many: 'Those with religious beliefs are surely right to consider that a national disaster is a test of their faith. On the abundant available evidence does it not seem that, if there is or was a God, it is now malevolent, mad or dead?'

Disaster by design?

Many other charges are levelled against God. Our planet can supply all our fundamental needs, yet teems with living organisms, from poisonous vegetation to viruses, and from killer sharks to bacteria, that can disfigure, dismember or destroy us. Even the air we breathe is sometimes contaminated with life-threatening agents of one kind or another.

Is this what we should expect of a God who '[gives] life to everything' (Nehemiah 9:6) and whose verdict on the whole of creation was that it was 'very good'? (Genesis 1:31). In a debate at the University of California at Irvine, Gordon Stein, then Vice-President of Atheists United, twisted the knife: 'If all living things on the earth were created by a God, and he was a loving God who made man in his own image, how do you explain the fact that he must have created the tapeworm, the malaria parasite, the tetanus germ, polio, ticks, mosquitoes, cockroaches and fleas?'

Accidents

The world-class scientist and theologian Sir John Polkinghorne has rightly said that we live in 'a world with ragged edges, where order and disorder interlace with each other', an assessment borne out in part by billions of accidents. Most are relatively trivial, but the outcome of some is so appalling that one word is enough to identify them years after the event concerned.

- When the British passenger liner *Titanic* was launched it was the largest and most luxurious ever built. Its owners boasted that 'God himself couldn't sink this ship', yet on her maiden voyage in 1912 she struck an iceberg in the North Atlantic and, in the greatest maritime disaster in history, sank with the loss of over 1,500 lives.
- On the night of 2 December 1984 the slums of the Indian city of Bhopal were enveloped in toxic gas released by accident from a pesticide factory. Over twenty tons of methyl iso-cyanate leaked into the atmosphere, its poisonous cloud burning the tissues of people's eyes

and lungs and attacking their central nervous systems. Many lost control of their bodily functions and drowned in their own body fluids. Nearly 4,000 people died within a few hours. Unclaimed bodies were driven by the truckload to burial- and burning-grounds. Another 16,000 of those poisoned that night died within the following twenty years, at the end of which time another 150,000 were still receiving regular medical treatment.

• On 26 April 1986 two explosions destroyed the core of Unit 4 in the RBMK nuclear reactor in the Ukrainian town of Chernobyl. The world's worst nuclear-power accident released radiation equivalent to a thousand times that of the atomic bombs that destroyed Hiroshima during the Second World War. Only thirty-one people were killed at the time, but ten million others living in twenty-seven cities and over 2,600 villages had to be evacuated from contaminated areas. Later estimates suggested that up to 800,000 Ukrainian children might be at a long-term risk of contracting leukaemia, while one report said it might take 200 years to remove the effects of the catastrophe.

These appalling accidents represent countless others: aeroplanes crash; trains are derailed; road vehicles collide; ships are lost at sea; buildings collapse; bridges give way; trees fall; machinery malfunctions. In hundreds of different ways, every day adds to the millions accidentally killed, maimed or injured.

How can all of this be part of the Bible's scenario in which a caring, controlling God 'works out everything in conformity with the purpose of his will'? (Ephesians 1:11).

Man on man

When we think of 'evil' in a moral sense we usually have in mind 'man's inhumanity to man' — and history teems with it.

- It has been estimated that in the last 4,000 years there have been less than 300 without a major war. Someone wryly called peace 'merely a time when everybody stops to reload'. Thirty million people were killed in the First World War alone.
- The figures for the Second World War are so vast that they have never been accurately computed, but they include six million Jews exterminated by the German dictator Adolf Hitler (he called them 'human bacteria') in the infamous Holocaust, part of his plan to build an Aryan 'super-race'. Men, women and children were gassed twenty-four hours a day in Nazi extermination camps, their remains scavenged for hair, skin and gold teeth to make cushions, lampshades and jewellery.
- Even the sickening bloodletting of two world wars did not mean the end of massive atrocities. Opponents of the Chinese dictator Mao Tse-tung's Cultural Revolution in China in the 1950s were executed at the rate of over 22,000 a month. In the 1970s, the Cambodian Marxist Pol Pot slaughtered over 1,500,000 of his fellow countrymen in less than two years. A savage civil war in Rwanda in 1994 claimed 800,000 victims, decimating the country and leaving nearly 350,000 orphaned children behind.
- '9/11' has become shorthand for the audacious terrorist attack on the United States on 11 September 2001. In a meticulously coordinated assault, two commercial aircraft on scheduled flights were hijacked and rammed into the twin towers of New York's World Trade Centre. Office equipment, human bodies and body parts were blown or sucked out of the buildings and rained down on to the surrounding streets 'like ticker tape'. Within ninety minutes the towers collapsed, setting off a huge mushroom cloud of yellow dust so massive and dense that it blotted out the sun. When the dust eventually settled, nearly 3,000 men, women and children lay buried under a hideous mass of rubble.

A third hijacked airliner had been steered into the Pentagon in Washington, D.C., killing nearly 200 people, while a fourth, in which passengers had bravely thwarted the terrorists' intentions, crashed into a field in Pennsylvania, with the loss of forty-five lives. It was the bloodiest day

in the nation's history since its Civil War, which ended in 1865, and the most devastating attack the world had ever known. Small wonder that an editorial in *The Times* called 11 September 2001 'the day that changed the modern world', or that the *Daily Mail's* Mark Almond wrote, 'History will never be the same again.'

• Before 1 September 2004 relatively few people had ever heard of Beslan, a small town in the South Russian republic of North Ossetia-Alania, yet a few days later there were no fewer than 10,000 'Beslan' sites on one internet search engine alone. The town was catapulted from obscurity to infamy when a squad of some thirty highly organized terrorists with links to Chechen separatists seized Middle School No.1, took more than a thousand hostages, mostly children, then planted explosive devices throughout the school. When Russian special forces stormed the building, the terrorists' response was to

Where is God?
Where is he?
Where can he be now?

massacre 350 of their captives, most of them children. Over 700 children and school staff were hospitalized and the whole nation was plunged into mourning. Western observers called it 'Russia's 9/11'.

How do these atrocities — and countless lesser ones — make any sense in the light of the Bible's teaching that God is 'a refuge for the poor, a refuge for the needy in his distress, a shelter from the storm and a shade from the heat', and a caring Sovereign who 'guards the course of the just'? (Isaiah 25:4; Proverbs 2:8). Many people make no attempt to do so. During the Second World War the British novelist H. G. Wells wrote, 'If I felt there was an omnipotent God who looked down on battles and deaths and all the waste and horror of this war — able to prevent these things — doing them to amuse himself, I would spit in his empty face.' The Jewish author Elie Wiesel survived the Holocaust and in his deeply moving book *Night* he told of some of its horrors — babies pitchforked as if they were bales of straw, children watching other children being hanged, and his mother and other members of his family thrown into a furnace fuelled by human bodies, while prisoners groaned, 'Where is God? Where is he? Where can he be now?' When it was all over Wiesel said that his experience 'murdered my God and my soul and turned my dreams to dust'. In a wider context the British art critic Brian Sewell confessed: 'After watching a world gone mad with greed and aggression … I ceased to believe in God and abandoned faith and its observance.'

Questions

For many people the case against God seems pretty watertight — but is it? Before building a biblical reply some critical questions need to be asked.

Why should issues of good and evil, or human suffering, cause any problems? If the British philosopher Bertrand Russell was right to dismiss man as 'a curious accident in a backwater', why should it matter in the least whether lives are ended slowly or suddenly, peacefully or painfully, one by one or *en masse*? If the Oxford professor Peter Atkins, another dogmatic atheist, is right to call mankind 'just a bit of slime on a planet', why should we be remotely

concerned at the systematic slaughter of six million Jews or half a million Rwandans? Are we traumatized when we see slime trodden on or shovelled down a drain? The whole world wept over the destruction and death brought about by the tsunami in the Indian Ocean, but why not have the same anguish over the fate of beetles or bacteria, rats or reptiles? If human beings are simply the result of countless chemical and biological accidents, how can they have any personal value, and why should we turn a hair if dictatorial regimes or natural disasters dispose of them by the million? The same applies to violence or bloodshed on a personal or limited basis. If we are nothing more than biological flukes, with no meaningful origin or destiny, why should the way we treat each other matter more than the way other creatures behave?

How can evolutionary development be a basis for morality and moral standards? The British scientist-turned-preacher Rodney Holder pinpoints the problem: 'If we are nothing but atoms and molecules organized in a particular way through the chance processes of evolution, then love, beauty, good and evil, free will, reason itself — indeed all that makes us human and raises us above the rest of the created order — lose their objectivity. Why should I love my neighbour, or go out of my way to help him? Rather, why should I not get everything I can for myself, trampling on whoever gets in my way?'

How can we jump from atoms to ethics and from molecules to morality? If we are merely genetically programmed machines, how can we condemn anything as being 'evil', or commend anything as being 'good'? Why should we be concerned over issues of justice or fairness, or feel any obligation to treat other 'machines' with dignity or respect? When people respond to tragedy by asking, 'How can there be a just God?' their question is logically flawed, as without him words like 'just' and 'unjust' are purely matters of personal opinion.

Far from moral problems ruling out the existence of God, our sense of things being right or wrong, fair or unfair, just or unjust is a strong clue that there is some transcendent standard that affects us all.

Where else, apart from God, can we find a basis for conscience, the mysterious moral monitor that wields such remarkable and universal power? Conscience is not to be confused with instinct or desire, as it often cuts across both, but where does it get its traction? We have already seen that nature is

neutral and has no moral values. Personal choice is also a non-starter, as it could justify any course of action, from the foulest to the finest. Society is no more reliable, as it is merely an amalgamation of individuals. On the other hand, our creation by an all-righteous God would provide a rational and logical basis for conscience and explain our sense of personal obligation. The distinguished geneticist Francis Collins, who led the successful effort to complete the Human Genome Project, makes the point well: 'This moral law, which defies scientific explanation, is exactly what one might expect to find if one were searching for the existence of a personal God who sought relationship with mankind.'

Asking and answering these questions points us to what some will find the strangest of conclusions: the existence of evil points *towards* the existence of God, not away from it! Getting rid of God does not solve the problem of evil and suffering; it merely leaves us trapped in what someone has called 'that hopeless encounter between human questioning and the silence of the universe'.

Here are children born with a congenital disease as a result of their parents' promiscuous lifestyle, a pensioner lying in a pool of blood after being savaged by a passing hooligan, a young mother who suddenly discovers that she has breast cancer, a successful businessman who notices the first signs of Parkinson's disease, distraught parents discovering their child is autistic, a pedestrian paralysed for life after being mown down by a drunken driver, a haemophiliac who has contracted AIDS by being infected with HIV during a blood transfusion, a frantic mother watching as New York's twin towers crumple, carrying her son to his death, a holidaymaker in Sri Lanka watching helplessly as his wife and children are swept away by a ferocious wall of water. Talk of a sovereign, loving God may not provide instant or totally satisfying answers to such people, but atheism is incapable of either explanation or consolation. Can thinking, feeling, hurting, grieving, questioning people live with this? Is it sufficient to tell the sufferers that tragedies and catastrophes are sick jokes and that truth, values and hope are figments of human imagination? Must we condemn hurting humanity to the total darkness that remains when God is discarded?

WHERE IS GOD WHEN THINGS GO WRONG?

Awkward facts

These are not the only questions that need to be raised. Others arise when we nail down some basic facts.

• Although our planet provides enough food to feed all six billion of us, millions die of starvation every year because of our selfish pollution of the atmosphere, our exploitation or mismanagement of the earth's resources and the vicious policies of dictatorial regimes. Can we blame God for these? Is he responsible for diverting disaster funds into the pockets of tyrannical rulers or greedy politicians? Millions are dying of hunger in India while its national religion forbids the use of cows as food. Hinduism has millions of man-made gods; can the country's chronic food problems be blamed on the one it ignores?

• Suffering is often caused by human error or incompetence. Had the owners of the *Titanic* not reduced the recommended number of lifeboats to avoid the boat deck looking cluttered, many more, if not all, of the ship's passengers might have been saved. Was God responsible for that executive decision? The International Atomic Enquiry Agency blamed 'defective safety culture' for the Chernobyl disaster. Can the blame for careless neglect of safety procedures be laid at God's door?

• A great deal of human suffering is deliberately self-inflicted. Smokers who ignore health warnings and are crippled by lung cancer or heart disease, heavy drinkers who suffer from cirrhosis of the liver, drug addicts and those dying of AIDS after indiscriminate sex are obvious examples. So are gluttons who dig their graves with knives and forks, workaholics who drive themselves to physical or mental breakdowns, to say nothing of the countless people who suffer from serious illness as a direct result of suppressed hatred, anger, bitterness and envy. Is God to blame for their behaviour? Can we point the finger at God when an air crash is caused by pilot error? Is he at fault when a drunken motorist causes an accident, a train is driven through a danger signal, or a ship's captain ignores safety procedures? Is God guilty when a person steps

carelessly in front of a bus? Is he responsible when a reckless tackle by a footballer ends an opponent's career?

The link between wrongdoing and its consequences is so clear that I want to make the point in a directly personal way. Ravi Zacharias tells of a discussion he and others had with an American business tycoon, who asked why God was silent when there was so much evil in the world. At one point someone asked the businessman, 'Since evil seems to trouble you so much, I would be curious to know what you have done about the evil you see within you.' There was what Zacharias called 'a red-faced silence'. How would you have responded? Are you doing everything you can to root out from your life whatever you sense to be less than perfect and to ensure that you do nothing whatever to add to the pain, suffering, misery and unhappiness in the world? If not, are you qualified to accuse God of mismanagement?

The Bible says…

The Bible says a great deal on the subject, but at no point does it offer glib or simplistic answers to solve all problems, end all pain and tie up all the loose ends. Instead, it says that with regard to the deepest matters of all, 'we see but a poor reflection' (1 Corinthians 13:12) in this life. Sceptics may see this as dodging the issue, but this argument is easily countered.

Firstly, the very existence of a truly transcendent God is a mystery. If we could understand all there is to know about God he would no longer be God.

Secondly, there is no logical basis for assuming that God owes us an explanation for anything that happens in the world. Can we seriously claim the right to know?

Thirdly, to say that the Bible does not tell us everything is not to say that it tells us nothing. Being left with doubts is not the same as being left in the dark. How could we know all the answers unless we had total knowledge of everything? To say that unless we see the whole picture there *is* no picture is

arrogance masquerading as intelligence. Even the strongest believer admits there are things in life that leave us with questions, not answers. Anyone denying this and trying to find a simplistic solution to all the questions raised by evil and suffering is on a fool's errand.

Fourthly, God says, 'My thoughts are not your thoughts, neither are your ways my ways. As the heavens are higher than the earth, so are my ways higher than your ways and my thoughts than your thoughts' (Isaiah 55:8); then how could we possibly understand everything God could tell us? There is a world of difference between the way we think and the way God thinks! Anybody who disagrees with this is suffering not merely from delusions of grandeur, but from madness.

Fifthly, while the Bible does not tell us all we *want* to know, it does tell us all we *need* to know, and on the issue of evil and suffering it takes us back far beyond all the instances of these things that we have discussed to tell us how it all began — and where it is all leading.

The stained planet

An article in *The Times* once asked, 'What's wrong with the world?' In the correspondence that followed, the shortest letter was by far the best:

In response to your question, 'What's wrong with the world?' — I am.
Yours faithfully,
G. K. Chesterton

The well-known British author's confession endorses the fact that when looking for somebody to blame for evil and suffering, nobody is in a position to point an accusing finger at God.

The Bible says that when God created the world it was without blemish of any kind, reflecting his own perfect nature: 'God saw all that he had made, and it was very good' (Genesis 1:31). Not a single molecule was out of harmony with God or with any other part of creation. Included in this perfect

universe was humanity, distinct from all the rest of creation in being made 'in the image of God' (Genesis 1:27), a phrase that tells us at least three things about man:

1. He was created as a personal being, capable of a living relationship with his Creator and with his fellow human beings.
2. He was created as a moral being, his conscience making him aware by nature of the difference between right and wrong.
3. He was created as a rational being, able not merely to think, draw conclusions and make sensible decisions, but specifically to make moral choices. Although moral perfection was stamped upon him at his creation, he was not a robot, programmed to do whatever God dictated. Instead, he had the ability to obey God and the freedom to disobey him. This state of perfection lasted until a created angel or spirit called Satan, who had previously rebelled against God's authority, persuaded Adam and his wife Eve to disbelieve God and disobey his clear directions. The moment they did so, 'Sin entered the world' (Romans 5:12) — with catastrophic consequences:

•   Man's relationship with God, which had depended on unqualified obedience, was shattered. Man retained his spiritual nature, but lost his spiritual life. He remained a person, but forfeited dynamic union with his Maker.
•   He lost his innocence and his moral free will, his very nature becoming infected with godless ideas, attitudes and affections.
•   His own personality was wrecked. He lost his self-esteem and for the first time knew what it was to be guilty, alienated, ashamed, anxious and afraid.
•   His interpersonal relationships were poisoned by suspicion, dishonesty, mistrust and the need to justify himself.
•   His body became subject to decay, disease and death, things that were never built into man's original make-up.

WHERE IS GOD WHEN THINGS GO WRONG?

Yet these disasters are more than ancient history, something we can read and then shrug off as irrelevant today. Adam sinned as the representative head of the human race and because humanity is an integrated whole he took the entire species with him: 'Sin entered the world through one man, and death through sin, and in this way death came to all men, because all sinned' (Romans 5:12). Tied into this is the fact that it was after his disastrous fall into sin that Adam began to father children 'in his own likeness, in his own image' (Genesis 5:3).

> Like poison dumped at the source of a river,
> Adam's polluted and depraved nature has
> flowed on to every succeeding generation.

Like poison dumped at the source of a river, Adam's polluted and depraved nature has flowed on to every succeeding generation. You and I did not begin life in a state of moral neutrality, but with sinful tendencies and desires waiting to express themselves in words, thoughts and actions. Does your own experience not confirm this?

Rebellion against a God of infinite goodness, holiness and truth is infinitely evil, and as a result of man's rebellion the entire cosmos was dislocated, leaving creation 'groaning as in the pains of childbirth right up to the present time' (Romans 8:22). For all its beauty, the world as we now see it is not in its original condition, but is radically ruined by sin. Earthquakes, volcanoes, floods, tsunamis, hurricanes, and the like, were unknown before sin entered the world, and the suffering and death they cause are ultimately due to man's contempt for God, his arrogant and self-centred rebellion against his Maker's authority.

But why should God have taken such an obvious risk in giving man moral freedom in the first place? Whatever the answer might be, it seems clear that not even an all-powerful God could give man freedom while guaranteeing that he would use it wisely. A person who is free and yet not free is a contradiction in terms, and not even God could bestow and withhold freedom at one and the same time. Yet to say that a flawless God could not possibly have arranged things the way he did is going too far, as 'his way is perfect' (Psalm 18:30).

How can we possibly prove that God was wrong to give man freedom of moral choice? Would creating robots have been wiser? Are we qualified to make this kind of judgement? How can we know God's reasons and purposes unless we know everything he knows? In his fine book *How Long, O Lord?*, the American author Don Carson writes that God's way of working 'defies our attempt to tame it by reason', then adds, 'I do not mean it is illogical; I mean that we do not know enough to be able to unpack it and domesticate it.' As finite, fallen creatures we need to swallow our pride, whatever the pain, and accept that God's ways are beyond our limited and flawed understanding.

Traumatic experiences often put this conviction to the test — but the test can be passed. A Holocaust survivor quoted in *The Times* by Dan Cohn-Sherbok said that during his time in an extermination camp he never once questioned

WHERE IS GOD WHEN THINGS GO WRONG?

God's action or inaction: 'It never occurred to me to associate the calamity we were experiencing with God — to blame him or believe in him less, or cease believing in him at all because he didn't come to our aid. God doesn't owe us that, or anything. We owe our lives to him. If someone believes that God is responsible for the death of six million because he doesn't somehow do something to save them, he's got his thinking reversed.'

An interfering God?

But would an all-powerful, all-loving God not intervene to prevent evil and the suffering it causes? We can begin answering that question by asking another: What kind of God would do this whenever *we* wanted him to? In a debate at the University of California at Davis, Edward Tabash called God a 'moral monster' and issued this challenge: 'If you are listening, and you are really there, show yourself right now… Do a colossal miracle… Show me something more than ancient hearsay to prove your existence.' When nothing happened, Tabash claimed to have proved his case — but he missed the point that a god who allowed himself to be ordered around in this way would be surrendering the very qualities that make him God. A god who jumps whenever anybody shouts, 'Jump!' exists only in fairy tales. Would we really want God to prevent things happening (or cause other things to happen) by manipulating the laws of physics in such a way that we would never know from one moment to another which had been suspended? If God tweaked the laws of nature billions of times a day merely to ensure every individual human being's safety, comfort or success, science would be impossible and, as the British author Francis Bridger points out, 'We should be reduced to such a state of physical, social and psychological instability that life would fall apart, paradoxically bringing even more suffering in its train.'

Many say that an all-holy God would intervene in moral issues in order to prevent sin — and not only the atrocities committed by the Hitlers, Pol Pots and Mao Tse-tungs of this world. Surely he would take action to prevent child abusers, rapists, drug-pushers, drunk-drivers, burglars, and the like, from

causing such terrible pain and suffering? Yet logically this kind of argument leads to the uncomfortable idea that in moral matters we would find ourselves reduced to the role of puppets, not responsible for a single word, thought or deed (good or bad).

It would also mean that we would not be responsible for any thoughts, words or actions that were the *indirect* causes of suffering. After my weekly game of golf I drive to pick up my wife from another appointment. Imagine that I am delayed by those playing in front of me, then find that I am running behind schedule. Dashing out of the clubhouse to the car park, I accidentally knock over another member who hits her head so violently on a concrete kerb that she sustains irreparable brain damage. How should God have intervened to prevent subsequent years of suffering? By causing the players in front of me to play better or faster? By making me choose an earlier starting time? By shortening the time it took me to shower and change after the game? By steering the lady into the clubhouse through a different door?

We recoil against the idea that God is utterly in control of things to the point at which we are robbed of every atom of independence or choice — *but this is not what the Bible teaches*! It repeatedly says that God decrees everything that happens, yet it also makes it crystal clear that he is neither the author of sin nor implicated in it. As we shall see later, it tells us that human beings are free, responsible and accountable moral agents.

A case history

The Bible's fullest treatment of the issue of evil and suffering is the story of a man called Job, who lived over 3,000 years ago. Rated 'the greatest man among all the people of the East' (Job 1:3), he was seriously wealthy and the father of seven sons and three daughters. What is more, he was 'blameless and upright; he feared God and shunned evil' (Job 1:1), yet in one terrible day he was hit by both natural disasters and the actions of evil men. Most of his 11,000 animals were stolen; the remainder were incinerated by a massive fireball; many of

his servants were killed, and his ten children perished when a tornado struck the house in which they were holding a party (see Job 1:13-19). Yet after this personal holocaust, Job 'fell to the ground in worship' and said:

Naked I came from my mother's womb,
　　and naked I shall depart.
The LORD gave and the LORD has taken away;
　　may the name of the LORD be praised

(Job 1:20-21).

This was an impressive declaration of faith in the sovereignty of God, but it did nothing to stop Job's suffering. His health began to deteriorate; he was covered with boils; his skin started to peel off; his eyes grew weak; his teeth rotted, and he was hit by a combination of fever, insomnia and depression. Those nearest to him turned the screw and his wife indirectly challenged him to commit suicide: 'Curse God and die!' (Job 2:9). An inner circle of friends began by being sympathetic, but soon changed their tune and told Job that his great suffering must be punishment for great sin.

From then on, Job rode an emotional roller coaster. In the depths of depression he wished he had been stillborn: 'Why did I not perish at birth?' (Job 3:11). On the crest of a wave he looked forward in faith to spending eternity in God's presence: 'I know that my Redeemer lives… I myself will see him with my own eyes' (Job 19:25,27). At another point he questioned God's justice in allowing the ungodly to 'spend their years in prosperity and go down to the grave in peace' (Job 21:13), while he was 'reduced to dust and ashes' (Job 30:19). There were periods when he felt that God was either distant or deaf. His friends kept up such a barrage of questions, advice and accusations that Job complained, 'Will your long-winded speeches never end?' (Job 16:3). Then came the decisive turning-point of the whole story — God spoke directly to Job.

God's response to Job's agonizing questions forms the Bible's fullest treatment of the issue of evil and suffering — yet it never mentions either! Instead

of giving Job a neatly packaged explanation, God took a very different line. Often by a series of questions, Job was reminded of the way in which the natural world pointed to God's overwhelming greatness and power, in contrast to man's dependence and weakness:

> Can you set up God's dominion over the earth?
>
> (Job 38:33).

> Do you have an arm like God's?
>
> (Job 40:9).

> Have you ever given orders to the morning
>   or shown the dawn its place?
>
> (Job 38:12).

> Do you send the lightning bolts on their way?
>
> (Job 38:35).

The closest God came to answering Job's questions directly was to ask:

> Will the one who contends with the Almighty correct him? …
> Would you discredit my justice?
> Would you condemn me to justify yourself?
>
> (Job 40:1,8).

God told him nothing about the cause of pain and suffering, but focused instead on man's response. The torrent of words poured out by Job's friends had done nothing to bring Job clarity, comfort or courage; they had been 'words without knowledge' (Job 38:2), but as God spoke to him he began to get things in their right perspective:

• God was in absolute control of the universe, and nothing could frustrate his eternal purposes:

I know that you can do all things;
   no plan of yours can be thwarted

(Job 42:2).

• He was in no position to argue with God, or to question his dealings with him:

I am unworthy — how can I reply to you?

(Job 40:4).

• He was not in possession of all the facts:

Surely I spoke of things I did not understand,
   things too wonderful for me to know

(Job 42:3).

• A living relationship with God was infinitely better than religious feelings or ideas:

My ears had heard of you
   but now my eyes have seen you

(Job 42:5).

• He should confess that he had been wrong to question God's power, justice and love and should humbly commit himself to him:

I despise myself
   and repent in dust and ashes

(Job 42:6).

There are important principles here. Job did not get detailed answers to his specific questions, but he learned to trust God even when he could not trace him. This was not giving in to fate but, as the Irish preacher Herbert Carson

movingly put it, he was responding 'like a child in the darkness gripped in his father's arms'. God does not give us all the answers we want, and to claim that he does is both cruel and absurd. As the Australian author Peter Bloomfield puts it, 'The last thing needed by hurting people is the voice of opinionated advisers who presume to interpret providence.'

One message that comes across very powerfully from Job's experience is this: it is less important to know all the answers than to know and trust the one who does. Laying hold on this can be a liberating experience. Some years ago my wife was being crushed by life-threatening clinical depression, which cruelly smothered her faith. There seemed to be no relief in sight when, twice in one week, people wrote to her in almost identical words, lovingly reminding her that God was under no obligation to explain anything that he caused or allowed to come into our lives. This did not provide cut-and-dried answers to our questions, but within a day or so the suffocating cloud had lifted and Joyce emerged with her faith renewed and deepened.

God's megaphone

In his well-known book *The Problem of Pain*, the universally respected scholar C. S. Lewis wrote, 'God whispers to us in our pleasures, speaks in our conscience, but shouts in our pains; it is his megaphone to rouse a deaf world.' Lewis was right. For many people, life is utterly self-centred. If God features in their thinking at all, it is merely as a vague emergency service to be called in when the going gets tough or when they have a particular need. Such people need reminding that we are not the centre of the universe, nor are we in control of the forces of nature. God often uses suffering of one kind or another to help such people realize the dreadful reality and power of evil, get their thinking straight, find a proper perspective in life and seek his help. Millions of believers over thousands of years bear testimony to at least six ways in which God brings good out of evil for those who trust him.

Firstly, *there are times when suffering develops confidence in God's transcendent wisdom*. When Job complained about his traumatic experiences,

God declined to give him a neatly packaged explanation, adding that he could charge God with being uncaring or unjust only if he could match his wisdom and power:

> Where were you when I laid the earth's foundation?
>   Tell me, if you understand…
> Will the one who contends with the Almighty correct him?
>   Let him who accuses God answer him!
>
> (Job 38:4; 40:2).

In Greece, I once met a blind believer who had had both legs amputated, yet he told me, 'I have no complaint against God. These legs belonged to him anyway, so he is entitled to do whatever he likes with them.'

Secondly, *God sometimes uses evil and suffering to provide a focal point for a believer's faith.* Living in Judah around 600 B.C., the prophet Habakkuk was baffled by God's apparent indifference in the face of the nation's moral degradation. Yet even when God made it clear that things would get a great deal worse before they got any better, Habakkuk testified, 'I will rejoice in the LORD, I will be joyful in God my Saviour' (Habakkuk 3:18). Nothing is ever out of God's control, nor does he have to resort to crisis management because circumstances have taken him by surprise. Peter Bloomfield has a powerfully relevant comment about this: 'There is no valid reason for doubting God. Notwithstanding the curiosity and weakness of man, our unanswerable questions, the gaps in our knowledge, and the endless pursuit of unrevealed things while ignoring the revealed things, God is wholly trustworthy.'

Thirdly, *suffering is meant to be spiritually productive.* One New Testament writer encouraged his fellow believers to cultivate a positive perspective in times of trial, and to realize that their faith would develop their perseverance and lead them to become 'mature and complete, not lacking anything' (James 1:3-4).

Fourthly, the Bible says *there is value in God's disciplining of believers* in that 'the corrections of discipline' are 'the way to life' (Proverbs 6:23). Elsewhere, it explains, 'God disciplines us for our good, that we may share in

his holiness,' and adds that, although 'no discipline seems pleasant at the time, but painful', it eventually produces 'a harvest of righteousness and peace for those who have been trained by it' (Hebrews 12:10-11). This goes right against the grain of a culture which puts personal happiness and self-indulgence at the top of its agenda, yet countless generations of believers have endorsed its truth.

Fifthly, *suffering reminds us of our physical frailty and of our dependence upon God*, teaching us that there is more to life than health and strength. When God did not grant his prayer for healing, the apostle Paul came to realize that his infirmity was not punishment but a form of protection — in his particular case, 'to keep me from becoming conceited' (2 Corinthians 12:7).

Sixthly, *trials divert our attention from the issues of time to those of eternity.* So much of our time can be taken up with trivialities such as fashion, sport, deciding where to go on holiday, choosing a restaurant or items for our homes, but when a major disaster hits the headlines, or a serious accident or illness strikes, these things suddenly become irrelevant, and we are often driven to think seriously about the certainty of our own death and of what might lie beyond. Sudden trauma often causes people to reflect deeply on the fact that 'What is seen is temporary, but what is unseen is eternal' (2 Corinthians 4:18). Herbert Carson gives a fine illustration of the right perspective to have: 'Slum clearance is not an end in itself … its ultimate aim is to move people to better homes. So in all God's dealings, which at times may appear harsh, he is gently and graciously preparing us for removal.' The Bible nowhere offers believers an insurance policy against suffering, but it does point to a way of coping with it by trusting God, who promises his people an eternal future beyond its reach.

When claims are made that an all-powerful God could overcome evil and that an all-loving God would do so, the person who believes in God agrees, but adds that as this is not happening at present we can be certain that it will happen in the future. In trying to look ahead, unbelief can only stare out into a hopeless void, where wrongs can never be righted and evil has the last word, but the Bible gives a very different perspective. It says that although God allows evil and suffering to coexist for a time, and for purposes we can never fully

understand, they will one day be eliminated and the problems they produce will be perfectly and permanently solved. The God who brought the present order of things into existence and who is 'sustaining all things by his powerful word' (Hebrews 1:3) will bring this devastated and degraded cosmos to an end and transform it into 'a new heaven and a new earth, the home of right-eousness' (2 Peter 3:13), in which there will be 'no more death or mourning or crying or pain', because 'the old order of things' will have 'passed away' (Revelation 21:4).

The day is coming when God will make a universal moral adjustment. Perfect justice will be done — and be seen to be done. The wicked will no longer prosper, the righteous will no longer suffer and the problem of evil will be fully and finally settled, beyond all doubt and dispute. This is what enabled the apostle Paul to brush aside twenty years of almost unremitting pain and pressure as 'light and momentary troubles' (2 Corinthians 4:17), and to assure his fellow believers, 'Our present sufferings are not worth comparing with the glory that will be revealed in us' (Romans 8:18). The existence of evil and suffering does not eliminate the possibility of God, but the existence of God guarantees for his people the elimination of evil and suffering.

If we confine our thinking to time and space alone we will never get to grips with the issue of evil and suffering. Answers to questions about meaning and purpose lie outside of the 'box' in which atheism operates. Just as the move-ment of the tides makes no sense until we know about the gravitational pull of the moon, so 'boxed-in' thinking can never find answers that will quieten our minds or satisfy our hearts. A biblical response to evil and suffering goes beyond time and space because it is rooted in a personal relationship with God, who is not an impotent spectator of human agony, but is in total control of everything that happens.

The man who was God

The Bible then goes a huge step farther and reveals that God has entered intimately into the reality of human suffering and at indescribable cost taken

radical action to punish evil and eventually to destroy it. He did this in the person of Jesus Christ. In the smash-hit musical *Jesus Christ Superstar*, Mary Magdalene sings, 'He's a man; he's just a man.' She was right — and wrong! The Bible certainly makes it clear that although his character, words and actions place him head and shoulders above the other sixty billion people who have ever lived, *he was truly and fully human.* As a child, he had to be taught to stand, walk, speak and write, and to feed and dress himself. He knew what it was to be tired, hungry and thirsty. Concerned at tragedy coming upon others, he 'wept' (Luke 19:41); on hearing good news, he was 'full of joy' (Luke 10:21). Even more significantly, he was 'tempted in every way, just as we are' (Hebrews 4:15).

Yet *he was more than a man.* Hundreds of years before he was born, prophets sent by God promised that he would one day intervene in human history by sending a great deliverer — the Messiah — who would provide the perfect answer to man's greatest need. There were over 300 of these prophecies, covering the time and exact place of his birth, his family tree, his lifestyle, his teaching, his miraculous powers, and minute details of the events surrounding his death. Even more amazingly, they said that he would be born of a virgin, something unique in human experience.

Jesus fulfilled every one of these prophecies to the letter, and in doing so endorsed the Bible's unanimous testimony that he was 'the image of the invisible God' (Colossians 1:15), and 'the fulness of the Deity … in bodily form' (Colossians 2:9). But why did he come? The Bible could not be clearer. He did not come as a politician, a diplomat, an economist, a scientist, a doctor or a psychiatrist, but to deal with mankind's most radical and deadly problem — what the Bible uncompromisingly calls 'sin'.

As we saw earlier, God's original verdict on creation (mankind included) was that it was 'very good', everything in it meeting with his unqualified approval. Things have changed! Today's media is clogged with reports of violence, bloodshed, debauchery, immorality, dishonesty, corruption, greed and sin of every kind — and the Bible relentlessly pinpoints the cause as being the depravity of the human heart, which is 'deceitful above all things and beyond cure' (Jeremiah 17:9).

The suffering Saviour

It is this horrific problem that God came to solve in the person of Jesus Christ — and in so doing he endured to the full the pain and suffering that sin causes. This has been powerfully expressed in these words, first written in the 1960s:

At the end of time, billions of people were scattered on a great plain before God's throne. Most shrank from the brilliant light before them. But some groups near the front talked heatedly — not with cringing shame but with belligerence. 'Can God judge us?'

'How can he know about suffering?' snapped a pert young brunette. She ripped open a sleeve to reveal a tattooed number from a Nazi concentration camp. 'We endured terror … beating … torture … death!'

In another group a black man lowered his collar. 'What about this?' he demanded, showing an ugly rope burn. 'Lynched for no crime but being black!'

In another crowd, a pregnant schoolgirl with sullen eyes. 'Why should I suffer?' she murmured. 'It wasn't my fault.'

Far out across the plain were hundreds of such groups. Each had a complaint against God for the evil and suffering he had permitted in his world. How lucky God was to live in heaven where all was sweetness and light, where there was no weeping or fear, no hunger or hatred! What did God know of all that men had been forced to endure in this world? 'For God leads a pretty sheltered life,' they said.

So each of these groups sent forth their leader, chosen because he had suffered the most. A Jew, a black, a person from Hiroshima, a horribly disabled arthritic, a thalidomide child. In the centre of the plain they consulted with each other.

At last they were ready to present their case. It was rather clever. Before God could be qualified to be their Judge, he must endure what they had endured. Their verdict was that God should be sentenced to live on earth — as a man! Let him be born a Jew. Let the legitimacy of his birth

be doubted. Give him a work so difficult that even his family will think him out of his mind when he tries to do it. Let him be betrayed by his closest friends. Let him face false charges, be tried by a prejudiced jury and convicted by a cowardly judge. Let him be tortured. At last, let him see what it means to be terribly alone. Then let him die in agony. Let him die so that there can be no doubt that he died. Let there be a whole host of witnesses to verify it.

As each leader announced the portion of his sentence, a loud murmur of approval went up from the throng of people assembled. When the last had finished pronouncing sentence there was a long silence. No one uttered another word. No one moved. For suddenly all knew that God had already served his sentence.

Evil, suffering … and you

These powerful words point to this stupendous truth: God understands our suffering because he has experienced it. He did so when in an act of indescribable love Jesus, the eternal Son of God, allowed himself to be put to death. The Bible makes it clear that 'The wages of sin is death' (Romans 6:23) and that, although he was absolutely sinless, 'Christ died for the ungodly' (Romans 5:6), voluntarily taking the place of sinners and in his own body and spirit bearing in full the punishment they deserved. In the Bible's words, 'Christ died for sins once for all, the righteous for the unrighteous, to bring you to God' (1 Peter 3:18).

Jesus came 'to destroy the devil's work' (1 John 3:8) and demonstrated that he had done so when three days after his execution (again in precise fulfilment of prophecy) he rose from the dead, a stupendous truth confirmed by hundreds of independent witnesses, the transformation of his followers from feeble cowards to fearless conquerors, the institution and growth of the Christian church and his dynamic influence in the lives of millions of people over the past two thousand years. Now, as the 'one mediator between God and

men' (1 Timothy 2:5), he offers the forgiveness of sins and a living, eternal relationship with God to all who turn from their self-centred lives and commit themselves to him as Saviour and Lord.

But where do natural disasters and acts of wholesale terrorism fit in? Jesus once reminded people of what at that time was a recent catastrophe, in which a tower in Jerusalem had collapsed, killing eighteen people. Brushing aside current speculation, Jesus asked (and answered) one question about the victims before adding an unmistakable warning to his hearers: 'Do you think they were more guilty than all the others living in Jerusalem? I tell you, no! But unless you repent, you too will all perish' (Luke 13:4-5).

The lessons are crystal clear. Some people see '9/11' as God's judgement on the United States, and the devastation

Headline-making atrocities are wake-up calls, warning us that evil and suffering are real, life is brief and fragile, and death is certain.

brought about by the 2004 tsunami as his wrath against the sins of those who lost their lives. But Jesus made it clear that we have no warrant for saying that the victims of these two disasters were the worst sinners in the two places concerned and that they deserved to perish while others were preserved. Nor are we entitled to accuse God of appalling misjudgement in randomly selecting thousands of people to die unjustly. Instead, we should accept that in his infinite wisdom he withdrew his protective hand and allowed such events to take place for purposes that are far beyond our limited understanding, but that included giving a warning of the judgement awaiting all who reject his claims.

If this sounds too harsh, let me urge you to reflect that it is only by God's mercy that *all* of humanity is not wiped out. The fact that 'All have sinned and fall short of the glory of God' (Romans 3:23) means that if he were to eliminate the whole of humanity at this moment neither his justice nor his righteousness would be compromised. If God were to dispense immediate and universal judgement you would not be alive to finish reading this sentence! You are alive at this moment only because, at least for the time being, God 'does not treat us as our sins deserve or repay us according to our iniquities' (Psalm 103:10). It is 'because of the LORD's great love [that] we are not consumed' (Lamentations 3:22).

Soon after the events of 11 September 2001, I was asked, 'Where was God when religious fanatics killed those 2,800 people?' I replied, 'Exactly where he was when religious fanatics killed his Son, Jesus Christ — in complete control of everything that happened.' This is the clear teaching of Scripture. Those who collaborated in the execution of Jesus are described as 'wicked men', yet his death was also according to 'God's set purpose and foreknowledge' (Acts 2:23).

Natural disasters and headline-making atrocities are wake-up calls, warning us that evil and suffering are real, life is brief and fragile, and death is certain. Even more loudly they urge us to prepare for a final day of reckoning, when 'each of us will give an account of himself to God' (Romans 14:12), who will 'judge the world with justice' (Acts 17:31). Yet, as 'nothing impure will ever enter [heaven]' (Revelation 21:27), we can be sure that on the basis of our

own thoughts, words and actions our case would be hopeless and we would be justly condemned to spend eternity in hell, consciously enduring the appalling punishment we deserved. This is exactly what Jesus meant when he warned his hearers, 'Unless you repent, you too will all perish.'

Now comes the best news you will ever read! On the basis of the death and resurrection of Jesus in the place of sinners, God the Judge is willing to settle out of court! If you will come to him in true repentance and faith, turning from sin and trusting Jesus Christ as Saviour, all your sin will be forgiven, you will have peace with God, and when your earthly life is over you will spend eternity in his sinless, painless, deathless, glorious, endless presence.

P.S.

The story with which we began this booklet did not end with a shrivelled, embittered quadriplegic. Two years after she broke her neck, Joni Eareckson was still in a state of deep depression, but gradually her spiritual vision cleared and her faith grew strongly and steadily. She also developed a remarkable ability to paint with a brush held between her teeth, and Joni's paintings and prints have become treasured collectables.

In 1979 she founded Joni and Friends, whose ministry, including a daily radio programme carried by over 1,000 outlets, has brought enormous help to thousands of people around the world. Another facet of the ministry has so far provided 25,000 wheelchairs to developing countries. Now married, Joni Eareckson Tada has received numerous awards from seminaries, colleges and other national and international bodies and her thirty or so books are shot through with a radiant faith in God that transcends all her pain and privations. Here are some examples:

My accident was not a punishment for my wrongdoing — whether or not I deserved it. Only God knows *why* I was paralysed. Maybe he knew I'd ultimately be happier serving him. If I were still on my feet, it's hard to say how things might have gone. I probably would have

drifted through life — marriage, maybe even divorce — dissatisfied and disillusioned… I'm really thankful he did something to get my attention and change me.

Today as I look back, I am convinced that the whole ordeal of my paralysis was inspired by God's love. I wasn't the brunt of some cruel divine joke. God had *reasons* behind my suffering, and learning some of them has made all the difference in the world.

In one of the thousands of meetings at which she has spoken in forty countries, she pinpointed the overarching principle that has sustained her through years of suffering: 'When we learn to lean back on God's sovereignty, fixing and settling our thoughts on that unshakeable, unmoveable reality, we can experience great inner peace. Our troubles may not change. Our pain may not diminish. Our loss may not be restored. Our problems may not fade with the new dawn. But the power of those things to harm us is broken as we rest in the fact that God is in control.'[1]

Seize the day!

The day before the terrorist outrage in the United States an American Airlines passenger noticed a member of the cabin crew breaking up ice with a wine bottle and expressed concern that she might hurt herself. The crew member was impressed by this and after they had talked for a while she accepted a Christian tract from him. Later in the flight she told him that this was the sixth such tract she had been given recently and asked, 'What does God want from me?' The man replied, 'Your life,' and then explained her need to get right with God. Less than twenty-fours later she was on the first plane to crash into the World Trade Centre.

As you close this booklet, let me urge you to think carefully about two things. The first is that God makes you this wonderful promise: 'You will seek me and find me when you seek me with all your heart' (Jeremiah 29:13). The

second is that this gracious promise has a closing date: 'Seek the LORD *while he may be found*; call on him *while he is near*' (Isaiah 55:6, emphasis added). That crew member had no idea that her particular closing date was a matter of hours away and her remarkable story is a sobering reminder that nobody can afford to play fast and loose with God's patience and assume that they can respond at their own convenience.

In his perfect holiness God hates sin, yet he is 'not wanting anyone to perish, but everyone to come to repentance' (2 Peter 3:9) and, in his great mercy, he pours out his love on all who genuinely do so. Then let nothing keep you back from calling upon him here and now, asking him to forgive you and to give you grace to turn from sin and commit yourself to Jesus Christ as your own personal Saviour. Discover for yourself that 'The gift of God is eternal life in Christ Jesus our Lord'! (Romans 6:23).

1. Quotations on pages 3-5 and 37-38 are taken from *Joni*, published by Pickering and Inglis, and *One Step Further* published by Zondervan Publishing House, both by Joni Eareckson Tada.

This booklet is based in part on John Blanchard's book *Is God past his sell-by date?* Contact your local Christian bookshop for a copy, or order one direct from the publisher:

Evangelical Press
Faverdale North, Darlington, Co. Durham, DL3 0PH, England

Evangelical Press USA
P. O. Box 825, Webster, New York 14580, USA

e-mail: sales@evangelicalpress.org

web: http://www.evangelicalpress.org

If you have come to trust in Christ through the reading of this booklet, we would commend *Read Mark Learn*, a book of guidelines for personal Bible study, written by the same author. This can also be obtained from Evangelical Press.

If you need further help, please contact the following address: